ON THE STEADFASTNESS
OF THE ORTHODOX CHURCH

St. Raphael of Brooklyn

On the Steadfastness of the Orthodox Church

Saint Raphael of Brooklyn

Uncut Mountain Press

ON THE STEADFASTNESS
OF THE ORTHODOX CHURCH

© 2024
Uncut Mountain Press

uncutmountainpress.com

Special thanks to Maher Salloum.

All images are in the public domain.

Scriptural quotations are emended to better reflect the original text.

Saint Raphael (Hawaweeny) of Brooklyn, 1860–1915.
On the Steadfastness of the Orthodox Church.—1ˢᵗ ed.

ISBN: 978-1-63941-064-4

I. Orthodox Christian History
II. Orthodox Christian Ecclesiology

CONTENTS

St. Raphael of Brooklyn

CHAPTER I

A Historical Perspective on the Steadfastness of the Orthodox Church of Christ[1]

If we skim through reliable history, we come to know that the Church of Christ, since its foundation until now, that is, in the course of about nineteen centuries, did not rest in any century from the great struggle against the many who war against Her and the numerous who resist Her, both Jews, pagans, heretics and atheists. At the same time, however, we also recognize that victory, in every place and time, was the ally of the Church's luminaries and will accompany Her until the end of days, according to the witness of Her divine founder, our Lord and God Jesus Christ, who built Her on the rock of faith in Him and said: "The gates of Hades shall not prevail against Her."

During the first three Christian centuries, the Jews and all pagan nations rose against the Church of Christ throughout the whole Roman Empire and stirred against Christians a terrible, intermittent war, such that the blood of thousands

---

1 *The Word*, Number 23, December 1, 1909, Year 5, pp. 441-444.

of Christian martyrs was spilled like rivers during those centuries. Despite all this, the Church remained steadfast in the struggle until She finally achieved a clear victory over all Her enemies, Jews and pagans, at the beginnings of the fourth century in the time of Saint Constantine the Great, Equal-to-the-Apostles, the first emperor of the Christians, when the Christian faith became the prevalent religion throughout the Roman Empire instead of the pagan religion. As a remembrance of this clear victory, the Church appointed a special feast on the first Sunday after Pentecost and called it the feast of martyrs or all saints.

No sooner was this external war ending than a second, internal war rose against the Church, that is, the war of heresies, stirred up by false teachers such as Arius, Macedonius, Nestorius, the Monophysites, the Monothelites, and finally the iconoclasts. This second war—which lasted twice as long as the first war—was no less vehement in terms of persecution, resistance, unrest and disturbances against the Church. But like that first, external war, which gave to the Church many champions such as Ignatius, Polycarp, Cyprian, George, Demetrius, Barbara, Catherine, and all the cloud of holy righteous martyrs of Christ, this second, internal war also revealed in the firmament of the Church a large number of luminaries and defenders of Her Orthodox Faith. These are the righteous Church Fathers and distinguished teachers such as Athanasius, Cyril, Basil, Gregory, John Chrysostom, John of Damascus the golden speaker, Venerable Photios, and all fathers of the seven Œcumenical Councils and the nine local councils, who affirmed forever the teachings of the Orthodox, One, Holy and Apostolic Church of Christ, and for whom, in remembrance of their great struggles in refuting the heretical, evil teachings and affirming the Orthodox teachings of the Christian faith, the Church appointed a special feast to be celebrated every year on the first Sunday of Great Lent, named the Sunday of the Triumph of Orthodoxy over all heretical teachings.

The One who built the Church on the rock of faith said that "the gates of Hades shall not prevail against Her," yet He also said that His Church will be troubled and fought against in this world until the end of ages and times. At the same time, as He also taught that victory will always be on the side of the sons of faith (see John 16:33), we see that no sooner was the war of heresies ended than a third war arose against the Church, from both inside and outside, incomparably more destructive and devastating than the first and the second. For **on one side**, there appeared the claim of the Roman popes concerning supremacy and headship over all Christian churches. This claim unfortunately caused many disorders and strong disputes that finally ended, in the middle of the eleventh century, with the split of the one Church of Christ into two great churches, Eastern (Greek, *Romios*, Orthodox—or the Church of the Œcumenical Councils) and Western (Roman, Latin, "catholic"—or the Papist church), and subsequently the separation of thousands, rather millions, from the second church, constituting many sects independent of each other, the Protestant sects. **On the other side**, the Mohammedan Islamic religion appeared in the Orient, and its followers—Arabs, Circassians, barbarians, Mongols, Tatars and Turks—started destroying the foundations of the Eastern Empire known as the Empire of the Romans or the Byzantine Empire, by seizing its provinces one by one until, finally, in the middle of the fifteenth century, they seized the capital of the empire and the foundation of the Eastern Orthodox Churches: the city of Constantinople. But despite all the distress, torments, and sorrows that the Orthodox Church of Christ endured because of this double third war (which is still raging now), we see that this Church remains—by the grace of Her Divine chief and Her only

Heavenly head, our Lord and God Jesus Christ—steadfast, growing, flourishing, bright in every place, and most fervently preserving the entrusted Orthodox Christian faith without addition or subtraction.

So is not the steadfastness of the Orthodox Church of Christ, despite all Her afflictions from the beginning until now—despite all the persecutions, resistance, distress, torments, sorrows and opposition—a crystal-clear proof and illustrious confirmation of the truth of what Her Divine founder said, that "the gates of Hades shall not prevail against Her"?

Although this third war is still, as we said, troubling the Orthodox Church of Christ, even if its vehemence has recently diminished somewhat—thanks to the constitutional provisions that were declared in all the Ottoman provinces[2]—we see the spark of a fourth war, with its thunders and lightnings, threatening the existence of all the Christian Church. That is, the war of the atheist groups who deny every religion. These are the materialists, Darwinists, socialists, anarchists, and all their ilk. But as the Church remained steadfast and unshaken in the first three wars, so will She be steadfast in this fourth war too—no matter how terrible it might be—and the Church will not come out of it except with the crown of victory and triumph adorning Her divine head.

Accordingly, if we ever see the godless sons of Cain sending thunder and lightning here and there against their brethren, the faithful sons of Abel, let us be assured that their lightning is like the lightning of their predecessors, a cloud with no rain nor water, and their thunder is nothing but the sound of a stormy wind that blows a little bit in the air and vanishes. As for the Orthodox Church of Christ,

2   Saint Raphael is most probably referring here to the Constitution of the Ottoman Empire that was declared in 1876, whereby Christians were represented in the Ottoman parliament. –Translator

just as She was, until now, steadfast against the stream of persecutions, resistance, distress, torments, and sorrows, so will She remain steadfast until the end of ages and times by the grace of Her Divine founder, our Lord and God Jesus Christ, who built Her on the rock of faith in Him and said that "the gates of Hades shall not prevail against Her."

The Ark of Salvation
Zographou Monastery, Athos

St. Paul the Apostle

CHAPTER II

Refuting Some Modern Claims
about the Teachings and Orders of
Our Orthodox Church[3]

Many Christian writers in our age, even some Orthodox Christians, often throw arrows of blame and criticism against our Orthodox Church for standing firm, from ancient times until now, in Her teachings and orders, within the boundaries set by the seven Œcumenical Councils during the first eight centuries of Christianity, never deviating at any time, neither left nor right. Verily, they are not even content with this type of criticism against the Church, where their accusations are often based on haughtiness and delusion, but they often go beyond these accusations and express their thoughts and opinions on reformation, which they learned by watching the coups and revolutions that they see happening in most kingdoms in the world, which they want to apply to the Church. Thus, they say that if the Orthodox Church operates in every place and time according to the law of progress, regularly rectifying

3   *The Word*, Number 2, January 15, 1909, Year 5, pp. 21-26.

and amending Her teachings and ancient orders, as civil administrations do with their legislation and orders, to make them suitable to the spirit of the age, She would reach, in the scale of progress and growth, that lofty level reached by all civilly developed administrations of our current age. She would even, by conforming to the age, make Her children, particularly those enlightened by the light of modern sciences, abide in Her ecclesiastic fold and under Her fatherly care, so that they would not feel the urge to move away due to Her old-fashioned teachings and orders which are not suited to the spirit of the age.

So how can we repel from our Orthodox Church these arrows of blame, which are often infected with the poison of vain claims and blasphemous teachings?

First, we say that their analogy between the Christian Church and the civil administration is a great mistake, because the Church is a divine order while the civil administration is a human order. The goal of the first is to help Her children grow spiritually and morally and to prepare them for everlasting life, while the goal of the second is to improve the external affairs of its members along with their financial situation. The means of the first are the Christian teachings supported by divine grace, while the means of the second are human legislation supported by compulsory force. For if every civil administration developed its legislation according to what suits the spirit of Christian law, it would have the Church as a strong ally, and this alliance between the Church and the administration would incur tremendous benefits and goods to the society.

Knowing this, let us examine our Orthodox Church first from the point of view of Her spiritual and moral teachings and from the point of view of Her ecclesiastic orders, to see if we can find something that can be amended or changed in accordance to the spirit of the age.

First:

If we first examine our Church according to Her spiritual and moral teachings, we find that all Her teachings are taken almost verbatim from the book of divine inspiration; therefore, they consist of divine religious truths. Since one of the most important characteristics of divine religious truths is that they are eternally the same, then the teachings of the Church are never susceptible at all to change and alteration, unlike human teachings which continually change. This characteristic of divine teachings, which sets them apart from human teachings, is what the Savior refers to in the Gospel: "Assuredly, I say to you, till heaven and earth pass away, one jot or one tittle will by no means pass from the law till all is fulfilled" (Matthew 5:18), and "Heaven and earth will pass away, but My words will by no means pass away" (Matthew 24:35). Likewise, when the Apostle Paul says to the Galatians, "Even if we, or an angel from heaven, preach any other gospel to you than what we have preached to you, let him be accursed" (Galatians 1:8), he exhorts us, on one hand, to keep the divine teachings without any change or alteration, and on the other hand, he warns us against listening to false human teachings.

Indeed, let us examine on one hand the **symbol of faith**, which briefly contains all the religious Christian dogmas, and on the other hand the **ten commandments**, which contain all moral teachings. Is it reasonable to apply to them any minor amendment or alteration? For that symbol of faith and these commandments are the foundations of all religious Christian dogmas, both spiritual and moral. Given that the source of all these teachings is divine revelation, i.e., the Holy Scriptures, which contain all that is required to the believing heart and to the good will, then if we dare to drop anything out of it we risk eliminating all of it. And if we are able to exercise discernment in human teachings and civil legislation, considering that one teaching is more important than another and one law is more compelling than another, and so on, we cannot do something similar in Christian teachings, whether spiritual or moral, because the Lord Christ, who handed down these divine teachings through His Holy Apostles, did not command us to adhere to some of it more than to others, or to preserve some of it as more beneficial. But on the contrary, He commanded us to adhere and preserve all of it, without any preference among the teachings, consistently with what the Apostle James teaches: "Whoever shall keep the whole law, and yet stumble in one point, he is guilty of all" (James 2:10). It is clear from this saying of the apostle that he who stumbles in one truth among the spiritual and moral Christian truths becomes guilty of all these truths. Even if somebody just wanted to impose preferences among divine teachings, making one truth more important than others, he will find that he will neutralize all of them. History is the greatest witness to the fact that if religious delusion does not have boundaries, but one delusion results in a second, and then in a third, it finally leads its holder to deny all religious truths. Our current age supports this historical witness, for we see many who wish to jettison the teachings of the Church and change them. One person demands that some teaching be eradicated because it is not important, another person says that some other teaching is difficult to be grasped by the intellect, yet another person wants to eradicate another teaching because it is not suitable to the spirit of the age, and so on, so that if we fulfill all these demands, we would be obliged to abolish all the teachings. Imagine!

Thus, is it reasonable for the Church to listen to worldly opinions and act accordingly, so that people say that She is following the spirit of the age? Absolutely not. Rather, reason and truth require that the Christian Church remain always as it was; and our Orthodox Church still adheres, and always will adhere, to what was handed down by divine revelation—that is, to religious truths, both spiritual and moral, that admit no change nor alteration at all.

Second:

If we examine our Church in terms of Her rites, splendidly structured and loftily conceived, which were defined and established during the era of the seven Œcumenical Councils in the first eight Christian centuries, such as the order of prayers, feasts, fasts, and all that is related to divine worship and Christian conduct—we find that any amendment or change is not possible either. **First**, because they share a common origin with all other Christian teachings, i.e., divine revelation, for their compiler, definer and organizer is the one, holy, catholic and apostolic Church of Christ during the era of its Œcumenical Councils. Since this one, holy and apostolic Church is "the Church of the living God, the pillar and ground of the truth" (1 Timothy 3:15), then all that it compiles, defines and organizes is divine, not human. Thus, no worldly command or human power is allowed to subject them to the least amendment or alteration. **Second**, because these ancient ecclesiastic rites are related to the religious Church teachings in the same way that an image is related to its origin and the body is related to the spirit, so that he who disdains or mocks these Church rites is like him who disdains Her very teachings. Besides, the rites of the Church are so strongly interrelated that any violation of one of them results in the violation of Her entirety. **Third**, and last, because these ecclesiastic rites are the only means of the descent of divine grace and the true evidence of the Christian way of life, and because they are the clear sign of the truth of the Orthodox Christian Church of Christ, Her correct worship, and Her compete readiness to fulfill the spiritual and moral needs of Her children, which are necessary for salvation.

So what is the reason and need to amend and change them? Is it to satisfy some or many of the propagandist writers of our age and their followers among the naïve faithful? But the Holy Church should not agree with people's opinions and their worldly proclivities; rather, the people should agree with the Holy Church, with Her holy teachings and orders. Or is it to alleviate the burden of the Christian way of life? But the true Christian is the one who lives by Christ's commandment: "If anyone desires to come after Me, let him deny himself, and take up his cross daily, and follow Me" (Luke 9:23)—that is, the one who does not run away from spiritual or bodily struggles that are beneficial for salvation, but endures them with all patience and thankfulness, imitating Christ who endured for us all sorts of spiritual and bodily sufferings.

Yes, each local church, among the Orthodox churches of Christ, has the right, under rightful necessity and circumstances, to bind and loose, or amend and change **modern rites and orders** that were put in place after the era of the seven Œcumenical Councils, but she cannot and has no right to amend or alter any of Her **ancient rites and orders** established and defined by the one, catholic, holy and apostolic Church of Christ during the era of Her Œcumenical Councils. By **modern rites and orders**, we mean everything that each local church established separately after the era of the seven Œcumenical Councils, in particular **special celebrations and orders** that do not oppose the spirit of ancient rites and orders. These **celebrations** include feasts of local religious events or apparitions of the Lord or the Theotokos or the angels, or of miraculous icons or new saints, particularly with the Russians who became Christians after the era of the seven Œcumenical Councils, where many saints appeared and were glorified by God through splendid miracles, whose memory the Russian church celebrates every year, whereas the rest of the Orthodox churches do not celebrate them, and so on. As for the **orders**, they are such as the manner of church administration, whether it is patriarchal or conciliar; the distribution of inheritance among the children of a deceased person (among males, females and the rest of the relatives); the acceptable degrees of relationship in marriages, whether beyond the fourth degree of separation, and so on; and with regards to clerical dress, the type of fasting regulations, etc. Each local church has the right to change and alter such rites and modern orders as are not confirmed in an Œcumenical Council, such as celebrating the holy light in the church of Jerusalem, which is a local celebration, and therefore the church of Jerusalem can change it at any time.

In summary:

Our Church, the Orthodox Church, is a true treasury containing all divine teachings and orders, and no human hand can change or alter the least thing in Her. No matter the circumstances, location, or time, or whether the people might fall behind or progress, She boasts in Her exclusive strong preservation of all divine teachings and orders since ancient times without the least addition or subtraction. For every faithful, who truly believes in the divine grace always dwelling in the one, holy, catholic, and apostolic Orthodox Church of Christ, does not demand or wish to perform the least amendment or alteration or abrogation or any such thing in the divine teachings and orders of the Church. But the false faithful or the unbeliever not only demands the amendment and alteration of the divine teachings and orders of the Church, and even the abrogation of some of them, but even demands their complete abolition. We saw in our times, particularly among the children of our nation and faith here in America, that some people who have the appearance of Christianity in their speech, writings or acts are no different than unbelievers. Had it not been for God's mercy and His long-suffering, that Christian appearance would have been erased as well.

St. Epiphanios of Salamis

CHAPTER III

Why Does the Church Not Allow the Woman to Be a Priest?[4]

In our generation, when socialist teaching and atheist opinions are prevailing almost everywhere, it is not strange if we hear some people objecting even to the affairs of God Almighty, saying, "Why did not God create the woman equal to the man in everything?"

These self-wise objections include, "Why does not the Church allow the woman to be a priest?"

We answer them that the Church does not allow the woman to be a priest not only for the many reasons that make the administrations of all nations and distinguished people forbid women from becoming soldiers, but also and more so because God Almighty Who created the man and the woman, by His Divine Wisdom, did not choose to give the woman the same rights that He gave to the man since the beginning of creation.

This issue is not new. A small sect appeared in the early third century, a branch of the Montanist sect, known as

4   *The Word*, number 2, January 15 1908, Year 4, pp. 27-32.

the sect of Pepuzians, named after the town of Pepuza in Asia Minor, who had the custom of having women also in the clerical levels and in all church roles, and who based this practice on the quote from the Apostle Paul: "There is neither Jew nor Greek, there is neither slave nor free, there is neither male nor female; for ye are all one in Christ Jesus" (Galatians 3:28).

Saint Epiphanius, however, bishop of Cyprus (born in 307 and reposed in 403), contested the validity of this custom that opposed the divine commands, saying in his book that refutes all heresies (*Panarion*): "If the women of these heretics are elevated to the episcopal and clerical levels beginning from Eve their mother, let them hear God's words speaking to Eve the woman: 'Your desire shall be for your husband, and he shall rule over you' (Genesis 3:16). Let them also hear the words of the Apostle Paul: 'I do not permit a woman to teach [in the Church] or to have authority over a man' (1 Timothy 2:12), 'For man is not from woman, but woman from man' (1 Corinthians 11:8), and 'Adam was not deceived, but the woman, being deceived, fell into transgression' (1 Timothy 2:14). Alas, how great are falsehoods in this world!"

Then Saint Epiphanius goes on in his aforementioned book, revealing the incompatibility of the woman with clerical service by irrefutable proofs from Scripture. He says, "Let us remember what was since the beginning until now. Since the beginning, since God created the world, never at any time has a woman offered sacrifice to God—Eve herself, though she had fallen into transgression, still did not dare to undertake such a further impiety (i.e., to become a priest). Not one of her daughters dared to commit such a transgression against the law (e.g. to become a priest; and if we review the Old Testament from its beginning to its end, we do not find any sign of the existence of a woman priest, nor in any age of all ages. . . . But I shall also go on to the

New Testament as well. If it were ordained by God that women should offer sacrifice or have any canonical function in the church, then the Virgin Mary herself would have been more adequate and more worthy than all men and women to have functioned as a priest in the New Testament. She was counted worthy to bear the king of all in her own womb, the heavenly God, the Son of God. Her womb became a temple, and by God's kindness and an awesome mystery was prepared to be the dwelling place of the Lord's human nature, who willed, according to God's love for men, to be incarnated for the salvation of the world. But it was not God's pleasure [that she be a priest]. She was not even entrusted with the administration of baptism—for Christ could have been baptized by her rather than by John. But John the son of Zacharias dwelt in the wilderness entrusted with baptism for the remission of sins (Luke 3:2-22), while his father offered sacrifice to God and saw a vision at the time of the offering of incense (Luke 1:11-12). Peter and Andrew, James and John, Philip and Bartholomew, Thomas, Thaddaeus, James the son of Alphaeus, Judas the son of James and Simon the Zealot, and Matthias who was chosen to make up the number of the Twelve—all these were chosen to be apostles, to perform the clerical service and offer the Gospel < throughout > the world, together with Paul, Barnabas and the rest, and with James, the Lord's brother and the first bishop of Jerusalem, [they were chosen] to be the stewards of the mysteries of God (1 Corinthians 4:1). Successors to the episcopate and presbyterate in the household of God (1 Timothy 3:15) were appointed by this bishop and these apostles, and nowhere was a woman appointed. Scripture says, 'Philip the evangelist had four daughters which did prophesy' (Acts 21:9), but they were certainly not priests. And 'Anna the daughter of Phanuel was a prophetess' (Luke 2:36), but not entrusted with the priesthood. For the words, 'Your sons shall prophesy, and your daughters shall dream dreams, and your young men shall see visions' (Joel 2:28 and Acts 2:17) required fulfillment[5]. . . . And the Word of God was incarnate of the Virgin Mary, but not in order to make women priestesses. For it was not God's pleasure that this be done with Salome, or even with the Virgin Mary herself, who is the mother of the Son of God. He did not permit her to administer baptism or bless the disciples, or tell her to rule on earth. He did not order the woman called the mother of Rufus (Romans 16:13) to advance to this rank, or the women who followed Him from Galilee (Luke 23:55), or Martha the sister of Lazarus and her sister Mary (Luke 10:38-41), or any of the holy women who were privileged to be saved by His advent and who assisted Him with their own possessions—or the Canaanite woman (Matthew 15:22), or the woman who was healed of the issue of blood (Luke 8:43-49), or any woman on earth."[6]

We add to the words of Saint Epiphanius that the book of Acts relates an incident where Christian women could very well have been given at least the right to care for their widowed sisters in the Church. For the holy apostles, after the Christians living among the Greeks complained to the Christians among the Jews that the widows of the former were neglected in the daily distribution, summoned the multitude of the disciples and said: "It is not desirable that we should leave the word of God and serve tables," i.e., to neglect the divine service to take care of distributing food and drink to the widows and the poor during the agape dinner after the divine service. Therefore, they decided to elect dedicated persons to serve the widows during agape dinners. But whom did they select for this simple ministry? Did they select even one woman? No, they selected "seven

---

5   *The* Panarion *of Epiphanius of Salamis*, translated by Frank Williams (Atlanta: SBL 2013), pp. 638-639 ('Against Collyridians'). —ED.

6   Ibid., p. 643.

men of good reputation, full of the Holy Spirit and wisdom" (Acts 6:1-6).

Then after the Church grew and multiplied, and the number of Her faithful increased, She perceived that it was wise to establish a function specific to women, and called it "the office of deaconesses," i.e., **the sisters who serve**. This, however, did not grant deaconesses any of the rights of the male deacons, e.g., to assist the priests and bishops during the Divine Liturgy and other divine services and ecclesiastical orders; but it did allow them to take care of keeping the order in the Church among members of their sex only, to attend the baptism of young girls and women in order to take off their clothes and to clothe them, to visit the sick and the wounded, to take care of the poor and the broken, and such works of Christian love and mercy that most Christian churches perform in our age, and thus they were eventually called "sisters of mercy." So the Church's **deaconesses** of old, who were replaced by the **sisters of mercy**, did not have any lesser right to or relationship with the priesthood service at all. For how can the Church give women the right of priesthood when the Bible forbids them even from speaking in the Church? "Let your women keep silent in the churches, for they are not permitted to speak; but they are to be submissive, as the law also says. And if they want to learn something, let them ask their own husbands at home; for it is shameful for women to speak in church" (1 Corinthians 14:34-35, cf. 1 Timothy 2:12).

As for those who demand that the woman be given what man has in terms of rights and public offices, they have no concern except exercising their concept of equality, even if its practice transgresses the divine commandments and civil laws. But we say to them, along with all vigilant scholars of literature and Christianity and the accomplished scholars of natural sciences, that their concept of equality is invalid, especially in the issue of equating the woman with the man in terms of public offices, whether religious or civil, since the woman is created to manage the house and nurture the children, not for the politics of the country and sovereignty over the people, whether religiously or civilly. And if we absurdly assume that women could leave housework and the nurturing of children and hold men's offices, becoming priests, lawyers, judges and soldiers, how would they be able to fulfill the duties of their office while being pregnant or mothers? Who would perform these public works during their pregnancy and childbearing? For we should not ignore these matters, because they are natural and necessary, and they are among the most important reasons that make the woman unfit for public offices, whether religious or civil.

Some people object to this, saying that history teaches us that some women held a noble public office and fulfilled it successfully, e.g., that there have been queens who were well-suited to such a role. So why, they ask, does not the Church allow them to become priests?

We answer by saying that we do not deny the fact that some women have held royal positions, during tsarist and imperial times, as was the case in England, Russia and Austria. But the ones who proved fit for this office were rather scarce, and the credit for their effective administration of the kingdom goes to the skills and expertise of their advisors, ministers and employees who were men, not women. Nevertheless, queens are rare and those who were fit for this role were scarce, and a rare occurrence does not become a law. Aside from this, all women who became queens received the royal office not as a right granted to their sex, but as a necessity brought about by the customs of royal succession in some European kingdoms in the Dark Ages, or as the famous German writer Riehl says, "The succession of a female to the throne was a custom of the Middle Ages, since at that time they considered all the kingdom to be owned by the royal family. Thus, if the royal family did not have a male heir, the administration of the kingdom was transmitted to a female member of the royal family. But as the meaning of the family and of the kingdom becomes clearer, so much clearer becomes the invalidity of the succession of a female to the throne and the necessity of its abolition."

In summary:

If the woman is not qualified to hold any civil public office, and what she has held so far was only thanks to men, so no doubt that she will also be unqualified to hold clerical offices, especially seeing that the Bible completely forbids this.

Julius Caesar

CHAPTER IV

The Reasons for the Difference Between Eastern and Western Calendars[7]

Everyone who looks at the **calendar**[8] that is published yearly throughout all Christian nations sees that there is now a difference of thirteen days in the beginning of the year between Eastern Christians and Western Christians—i.e., that the first day of January on the Eastern calendar is the fourteenth day of January on the Western calendar.

This difference is due to the fact that the Eastern Church follows the old calendar, called the Julian calendar, while Westerners follow the new or Gregorian calendar.

---

7   *The Word*, Number 5, March 1, 1908, Year 4, pp. 86-90.

8   For nearly all Europeans, the calendar is the name of a book containing the account of the days and months in a given year, and what occurs within it of feasts and meteorological and astronomical changes and whatnot. It is derived from the Latin name **Calendarius**, which is derived from **Calendae**, meaning the first day of each month. Turks call such book "Rooznamah," a name composed of two Persian words. The first, "rooz," means "day," and the second, "namah," means book or calculation. The Syrians adopted the name "tak'weem."

The Julian calendar was named after its compiler, Julius Caesar, in 45 B.C. The astronomers at that time thought that the earth's yearly revolution around the sun—or the sun's yearly revolution around the earth, as they thought at that time—has a duration of 365 days and one-fourth of a day, i.e., six hours. Since the one-fourth of a day becomes one full day every four years, Julius Caesar commanded to add, after every three years, one full day to the month of February of the fourth year, so that the number of days in three consecutive years is 365 days, whereas in the fourth year it is 366 days. The Romans named this fourth long year *bissextus*, i.e., the year of two sixes, due to the existence of two sixes in the number of its days.[9] Whereas the Nazarenes of the East adopted the name "*kabeessah*," which means "packed," due to the "packing of the year with one additional day" (see *Muh'eet' al Muh'eet'*).

In order to know if the year is a leap year or a common year according to the Julian calendar, we have to divide it by the number four. If the remainder is zero, then it is a leap year; otherwise it is a common year. For example, the current year, 1908, is a leap year because it is divisible by four without any remainder, whereas next year, 1909, is common because it is not divisible by four without remainder, and so on. In general, each fourth year before or after the current year is a leap year, i.e., the number of its days is equal to 366, for the days of February therein is equal to twenty-nine days instead of twenty-eight days as in a common year.

This Julian year is actually slightly longer than the astronomical year, because the first consists of 365 days and six hours, whereas the second consists, according to most astronomers, of 365 days, five hours, forty-eight minutes and forty-six seconds. Accordingly, the Julian year is eleven minutes and fourteen seconds longer than the astronomical

---

9   In English, a *bissextus* year is called a leap year, and a year of 365 days is called common year. —Translator

year. This minor increase in the Julian year constitutes, every 400 years, three complete days, two hours, fifty-three minutes and twenty seconds.

Since the Julian calendar started in the middle of the century before the first Christian century, the increase therein reached, until the end of the fourteenth century A.D., ten complete days. So when Pope Gregory XIII (who ascended the papal throne in 1572 and died in 1585) learned of this increase in the Julian year over the astronomical year, based on the results of the research performed by Lilius, the famous astronomer who died in 1576, he determined to eliminate the increase from the Julian calendar and thus commanded that Friday 15 October 1583 be reconstituted as 5 October 1583. Thus, the spring equinox returned to the twenty-first day of March, as it was during the days of the first Niceaen Œcumenical Council, which defined the feast day of Pascha based on the thought that the spring equinox always occurs on the twenty-first day of March. Since the increase in the Julian year reaches, as previously mentioned, about three complete days every 400 years, to avoid this increase Pope Gregory commanded that the last year every fourth century, starting in the year 1700, is to be considered a leap year, while before the fourth century, i.e., in the years 1700, 1800 and 1900, these years should be considered common years. Since the years 1700, 1800 and 1900, according to the rule previously mentioned, are leap years in the Julian calendar (because they are divisible by four without remainder), the difference between the Julian calendar and Pope Gregory's calendar, at the end of the sixteenth century, was ten days only. Then it became, in the year 1700, eleven days, in the year 1800, twelve days, and in the year 1900, thirteen days. Since the year 2000 is the end of the fourth century after the year 1700, it is a leap year according to both calendars; therefore, the difference will remain thirteen days until the year 2100, when it will become fourteen days. In the year 2200 it will become fifteen days; in the year 2300 it will become sixteen days, and it remains as such until the year 2500, when it becomes seventeen days, and so on.

In order to know if the year is a leap year or a common year according to this new calendar, called Gregorian, we have to recognize its ones and tens. So if its ones and tens are non-zero numbers, we apply the Julian rule previously mentioned, i.e., dividing the year by four, and if there is no remainder, the year is a leap year; otherwise, it is common. But when its ones and tens are zeros (e.g., years 1700, 1800, 1900, 2000, etc.), if it is divisible by 400 without remainder (e.g., 2000, 2400, etc.) then it is a leap year; otherwise, it is a common year, such as the years 1700, 1800, 1900, 2100, and so on.[10]

The old calendar, i.e., the Julian calendar, is also called the **eastern calendar**, given that more people use it in the Orient, especially, the people of the Eastern Orthodox Church in all places, whereas the new calendar, i.e., the Gregorian, is also called the **western calendar**, given that all the people in the West use it, especially the people of the western catholic church and all the people of the Protestant churches as well.

So from what is mentioned until now, it follows that the year according to the western calendar is closer to the astronomical year than is the year according the eastern calendar. Despite this, it does not completely match the astronomical year, because after skipping three days every 400 years, as we saw, it still exceeds the astronomical year

---

10 Some think that a leap year signifies that the feast of Pascha occurs on the same Sunday on both the eastern and the western calendar. They should know that the leap year is not related to the feast of Pascha at all. For it can be a common year with Pascha occuring on the same day on both calendars. It may also be a leap year with Pascha not occuring on the same day, as in the current year 1908.

every 400 years, by two hours, fifty-three minutes and thirty seconds, i.e., by about three hours.

Now, if some say, "Why does the Orthodox Church not abandon the Julian calendar and follow the Gregorian calendar which, anyhow, matches the astronomical year better than the first?" We answer them with what the head of the church of Constantinople, Joachim III, said in his last letter to the Holy Russian Synod on May 12, 1904, which we published in Arabic in the fifth issue of our magazine, in its second year, on page 91. He said: "With respect to our eastern calendar known as the Julian calendar, we see that this calendar, affirmed and recognized in our Church since ancient times until now, and which requires that we celebrate the glorious resurrection of the Lord on the first Sunday or the following Sunday after the lunar full moon corresponding to the spring equinox, should be strongly preserved by us, without incurring the slightest alteration or modification therein. As for the opinion of some people that we should preserve our Julian calendar and the days of our feasts as they are but skip thirteen days so that the days of our months match the days of the months of the other calendar (i.e., the Gregorian), it is vain and not beneficial at all. First, because skipping a given number of days has no ecclesiastic or scientific justification. Second, because the agreement between the days of our eastern months and the days of the western months would be temporary, i.e., until the year 2100, when the difference becomes again one day. We also do not favor now the opinion of those who say that we must reform our Julian calendar because it does not agree with scientific findings, and that we must adopt a midmost civil year that better agrees with the astronomical year than both eastern and western calendars, because we are not in an urgent need to ecclesiastically change our calendar—let alone that, as experts confirm, science is still not able to know the astronomical year with full accuracy."

St. Constantine the Great, Equal to the Apostles

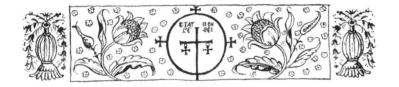

CHAPTER V

The Reasons for the Difference
in the Date of Pascha
between Eastern and Western Christians[11]

Since this year the glorious feast day of Pascha, for us Orthodox, occurs five full weeks after the western Pascha, many asked us what may be the reason that Pascha does not always occur on the same day on both eastern and western calendars. After all, we see that on some years, such as this past year (1909), they celebrate Pascha on the same day as us, while in other years, such as the year 1908, the difference is one week, in others, such as the year 1902, the difference is four weeks, and finally in some others, such as this present year 1910, the difference is five weeks.

We answer them that the reason is the firm preservation, on the part of our Orthodox Church, of the commands of the fathers of the First Holy Œcumenical Council, convened at the command of the holy emperor and Equal to the Apostles, Constantine the Great, in the city of Nicaea in the

11 *The Word*, Number 9, May 1, 1910, Year 6, pp. 168-173.

year A.D. 325, which, fulfilling this emperor's desire for true worship, that the holy feast of Pascha be one Sunday for all Christians throughout the world, established during one of their sessions a special canon explaining the method by which the date of holy Pascha was to be determined every year. Although the acts of this council (except its twenty canons) are lost, the ecclesiastical authorities preserved the paschal canon, which was handed down by the council and which has been observed since that time until now in our Orthodox Church.

According to this canon, we have to preserve three conditions when determining the date of holy Pascha, as follows.

First condition: the feast of Pascha must always occur on **the first Sunday after the full moon that is after the spring equinox**.[12]

For example, in the past year 1909, when the full moon after the spring equinox (i.e., after March 21, Eastern) occurred on Monday, March 23 Eastern (April 5 Western), the first Sunday after this spring equinox's full moon occurred on March 29 Eastern (April 11 Western), and the Easterns celebrated Pascha with the Westerns.

Second condition: the Sunday of Pascha must not occur before March 22 Eastern or after April 25 Eastern.

For in the current year 1910, since the full moon occurred on Friday March 12 Eastern (March 25 Western), the Westerners celebrated their Pascha on the first Sunday after this full moon, i.e., on March 14 Eastern (March 27 Western). But the Eastern Church did not celebrate Pascha with them because March 27 Western is March 14 Eastern,

---

12   The spring equinox is that day in the month of March when day and night are of equal length, when both consist of twelve hours. Since the spring equinox, at the time of the First Œcumenical Council, occurred on March 21, the fathers of this council appointed this day to be considered the day of the spring equinox.

and according to the command of the first Œcumenical
Council, Pascha should not be celebrated before March
22 (Eastern), i.e., before the spring equinox. Therefore,
the Eastern Church postponed its Pascha until after the
following full moon, i.e., the full moon of the month of
April. Since the full moon of April occurred on Sunday
April 11 Eastern (April 24 Western), and since Pascha must
be on the first Sunday after the full moon (first condition),
Pascha must be postponed until the next Sunday (which
occurs on April 18 Eastern, or May 1 Western), and thus
the difference between the Eastern and Western Paschas
becomes five full weeks. Likewise, in the year 1902, the
difference between the two Paschas was four weeks, not five,
due to the reasons previously explained regarding the year
1910, except the last, that the full moon of April 1902 did
not occur on a Sunday and therefore the Eastern Pascha
was not postponed until the Sunday after and the difference
was four weeks only.

**Third condition: The Christian feast of Pascha
must not coincide with the day of the Jewish
passover.** Therefore, if the Jewish passover occurs on a
Sunday then the Eastern Church postpones Her Pascha
until the following Sunday, while Westerners do not observe
this third condition.

For in the year 1908, the full moon occurred on Friday
April 3 Eastern (April 16 Western), and thus it was necessary
(according to the first and second conditions) to celebrate
Pascha on Sunday April 6 Eastern (April 19 Western), as
the Westerners celebrated it. But since the passover of the
Jews occurred between April 3 and 10 Eastern, and since
the Christian Pascha should not be celebrated at the same
time as the passover of the Jews (according to the third
condition), therefore the Eastern Church postponed Her
Pascha until the following Sunday (April 13 Eastern, April

26 Western), and the difference between the two Paschas was one week.

Therefore,

The reason for the difference in the celebration of the Sunday of Pascha between East and West is the Eastern preservation of the three conditions established by the First Holy Œcumenical Council concerning the celebration of the glorious Pascha: **first**, the necessity of celebrating Pascha always on the Sunday that occurs after the spring equinox's full moon (i.e., after March 21 Eastern). **Second**, the necessity of not celebrating Pascha before March 22 or after April 25 (Eastern). And **third**, the necessity of not celebrating Pascha on the same day as the Jewish passover.

For, since the First Œcumenical Council

is the one which defined the issue of the celebration of Holy Pascha, and as our Orthodox Church still preserves this tradition completely without addition or subtraction and with no change or amendment, we confirm this from the content of the first canon of the holy local council of Antioch, convened sixteen years after the first Œcumenical Council, i.e., in the year A.D. 341. That canon reads: "Whosoever shall presume to set aside the decree of the holy and great Synod which was assembled at Nicaea in the presence of the pious Emperor Constantine, beloved of God, concerning the holy and saving feast of Pascha; if they shall obstinately persist in opposing what was [then] rightly ordained, let them be excommunicated and cast out of the Church; this is said concerning the laity. But if any one of those who preside in the Church, whether he be bishop, presbyter, or deacon, shall presume, after this decree, to exercise his own private judgment to the subversion of the people and to the disturbance of the churches, by celebrating Pascha [at the same time] with the Jews, the holy Council decrees that he shall thenceforth be an alien from the Church, as one who not only heaps sins upon himself, but who is also the cause of destruction and subversion to many; and it deposes not only such persons themselves from their ministry, but those also who after their deposition shall presume to commune with them."

And since Pascha

must always be celebrated, not only after the spring equinox but also after the Jewish passover, this is also plainly confirmed by the seventh canon of the Holy Apostles, which says: "If any Bishop, or Presbyter, or Deacon celebrate the holy day of Pascha before the vernal equinox, with the Jews, let him be deposed" (see also Canon 70 of the Apostles, the first canon of the local council of Antioch, and canon 37 of the local council of Laodicea).

One might ask:

Why did the Holy Fathers ordain that the holy Pascha should be, first, after the spring equinox, not before it; and second, after the Jewish passover, not before it or with it?

We answer the first question saying:

Since the spring equinox is the cut-off point that divides the year into two halves, if we celebrate Pascha before the spring equinox, then we celebrate it twice within one year; thus we portray the death of the Son of God twice. But if we celebrate Pascha after the spring equinox, we carry out one Pascha per year and thus portray the death of Christ only once. This is why the Apostles said the following in their Apostolic Constitutions: "It is therefore your duty, brethren, who are redeemed by the precious blood of Christ, to observe the days of the passover exactly, with all care, after the vernal equinox, lest you be obliged to keep the memorial of the one passion twice in a year. Keep it once only in a year for Him that died but once" (Book 5, Section 17).

As for the second question,

why it is not right to celebrate the Christian Pascha before the Jewish passover or along with it, but only afterwards. The answer is, first, so that the image, which is the slaughter of the lamb, might precede that which it depicts, which is the death of the Lord and His resurrection. Second, so that we do not repeat Pascha on any day of the week (as the Jews celebrate their passover on any day on which the lunar fourteenth of April might occur) but always on a Sunday. Therefore, if the Jewish passover occurs on a Sunday, we celebrate our Pascha on the following Sunday so that we do not celebrate with them, because Jews, in the year when they crucified Christ, celebrated their passover first, before the resurrection of the Lord took place. Since the Christian Pascha is the remembrance of this resurrection, it is necessary that it should always be after the Jewish passover.

We said in a previous footnote

that when the fathers of the First Œcumenical Council defined the issue of Paschal celebration, the spring equinox occurred on March 21. Even though the date of this spring equinox changed afterwards, and receded until it now occurs on March 8, our Orthodox Church, respecting what the fathers of the First Œcumenical Council defined, still considers March 21 to be the day of the spring equinox. Her argument is that the Fathers of all the other Œcumenical and Local Councils that convened after the First Œcumenical Council, as well as all holy fathers, recognized with no doubt that the date of the spring equinox has changed from its occurrence in the time of the First Œcumenical Council; however, they did not dare to transfer it from March 21 but preferred to keep it as handed down by the ancient fathers—out of a desire to preserve the continuity of the agreement among the holy churches of God with respect to the celebration of the glorious day of Pascha instead of following the astronomical accuracy of the occurrence of the spring equinox. Besides, if we in the Eastern Church wished to follow astronomical accuracy in this regard, as the Westerners did,[13] we would fall into two of the same mishaps into which they have fallen. For after changing their calendar, they started celebrating Pascha with the Jews sometimes, which is plainly forbidden by the seventh apostolic canon, and sometimes before the Jews, which is contrary to the intent of the glorious day of Pascha, for then what is depicted precedes the image, and the Lord's resurrection precedes His crucifixion by the Jews.

We end our article.

---

13 The Westerners preserved the calendar now known as the Eastern calendar (now followed only by all the Eastern Orthodox Church-es) until the end of the sixteenth century, when Pope Gregory XIII commanded, in the year 1582, that ten days of that year be dropped from the month of October. He considered its fifth day as the fifteenth in order to correct the error that had been increas-ing since the time of the First Œcumenical Council (i.e., since the beginning of the fourth century until the end of the sixteenth cen-tury). In order to avoid this mistake afterwards, the Westerners re-sorted to considering the last year after a full century (e.g. the years 1700, 1800, 1900, etc.) as a common year, not a leap year, as the Eastern Church considers it. By the end of the seventeenth century, this resulted in the difference between the Eastern calendar and the Western calendar being ten days. It then became, in the beginning of the eighteenth century until its end, eleven days, and in the be-ginning of the nineteenth century until its end, twelve days, and in the beginning of the present twentieth century, thirteen days. Thus the difference has been increasing one day each century between the two calendars.

with what the reverent Church father and teacher of the universe, Saint John Chrysostom, said in his sermon "To Those Fasting": "The Church of Christ knows no accuracy of times or observation of days, since as often as She eats this life-creating Bread and drinks this cup, She is denouncing the death of the Lord and is celebrating Pascha. But inasmuch as the Fathers assembled at the First Œcumenical Council and ordained how to reckon the date of Pascha, because the Church honors agreement and union everywhere, She accepted the regulation which they provided. Though the Church does not hold to the timekeeping accuracy of modern times, no so great good could result from this accurate keeping of the time as the great evil which would ensue from this division and the schism from the Orthodox Catholic Church. For God and the Church do not seek provision for any so accurate observation of times and days, but confine their attention to fostering oneness of mind and peace . . . . But to divide the Church and form resistance and quarreling against Her, and to cause dissensions and divisions, and to separate oneself from the common convention of the Church, is an unpardonable sin, and one deserving to be denounced and entailing much punishment and castigation."[14]

14   See the book of canons known as the *Pedalion*, page 5, in the inter-
pretation and footnote of the seventh apostolic canon.

CHAPTER VI

Consolation from Saint Nicolas Khashsha[15] upon the Falling Asleep of Saint Raphael Hawaweeny in 1915.

From the book: "The Affections of the Children toward the Most Benevolent among Hierarchs and most Affectionate among Fathers" (A'watif al abnaa' nah'wa khayr al roo'assaa' wa a'ataf al 'abaa'), Archdeacon Emmanuel Abou Hatab, 1915, pages 286-287.[16]

With unsurpassed sadness and with many flowing tears, that are in the same measure of the love we have for you, I received the tragic news of the departure of Master Raphael, the support of the faithful, that pure angel whom time withheld me from meeting in this world to receive a blessing; perhaps it will join us in Eternity.

---

15 The holy father Nicolas Khashsha and his son, the holy father Habib Khashsha, were recently glorified by the Holy Synod of the Patriarchate of Antioch in October 2023. —Translator

16 This book was written in Arabic by Archdeacon Emmanuel Abou Hatab, a disciple of Saint Raphael. It contains the life of Saint Raphael as well as the description of his funeral service and all poems and letters of eulogy and consolation sent by the multitude of people, clergy and hierarchs who knew him. —Translator

What a great catastrophe! What a massive disaster! Does Orthodoxy lack this gaping wound? Are not Her ordeals and decline enough, while She looks beyond the seas to this great master placing high hopes in him? They faded, alas, my grief! After his delicate body survived that illness, and we rejoiced in the fulfillment of our desire, the days of sorrow and difficulty would not end, and then the illness returned and defeated that worn out body, smiting him as a martyr.

Oh my dear! Should I console you or console myself, or rather console the whole of Orthodoxy for this substantial loss, the loss of Her defender and support? Did not sadness overcome all the Orthodox world, both east and west? Who has not heard of Bishop Raphael Hawaweeny? Who denies his labors and glorious contributions? This last contribution is before us, this unique book, the great *Euchologion*.

I have no doubt that he has received joy seeing his Master, Teacher and Redeemer saying him, "Well done, good and trustworthy servant."

On my behalf, console whomever you wish.

The people of Mersin[17] join me with these emotions, and the next Sunday, April 16 (Eastern), is appointed for the funeral service at Saint Michael Church.

---

17 Mersin is a large town in southern Turkey on the Mediterranean sea. It is the town where Saint Nicolas Khashsha was martyred. — Translator

St. Nicolas Khashsha

UNCUT MOUNTAIN PRESS TITLES

Books by Archpriest Peter Heers

Fr. Peter Heers, *The Ecclesiological Renovation of Vatican II: An Orthodox Examination of Rome's Ecumenical Theology Regarding Baptism and the Church*, 2015

Fr. Peter Heers, *The Missionary Origins of Modern Ecumenism: Milestones Leading up to 1920*, 2007

Fr. Peter Heers, *Formation in the Love of Truth: Principles of Orthodox Education*, 2024

The Works of our Father Among the Saints, Nikodemos the Hagiorite

Vol. 1: *Exomologetarion: A Manual of Confession*

Vol. 2: *Concerning Frequent Communion of the Immaculate Mysteries of Christ*

Vol. 3: *Confession of Faith*

Other Available Titles

Elder Cleopa of Romania, *The Truth of our Faith*

Elder Cleopa of Romania, *The Truth of our Faith, Vol. II*

Fr. John Romanides, *Patristic Theology: The University Lectures of Fr. John Romanides*

Demetrios Aslanidis and Monk Damascene Grigoriatis, *Apostle to Zaire: The Life and Legacy of Blessed Father Cosmas of Grigoriou*

Protopresbyter Anastasios Gotsopoulos, *On Common Prayer with the Heterodox According to the Canons of the Church*

Robert Spencer, *The Church and the Pope*

G. M. Davis, *Antichrist: The Fulfillment of Globalization*

Athonite Fathers of the 20th Century, Vol. I

St. Gregory Palamas, *Apodictic Treatises on the Procession of the Holy Spirit*

St. Hilarion (Troitsky), *On the Dogma of the Church: An Historical Overview of the Sources of Ecclesiology*

Fr. Alexander Webster and Fr. Peter Heers, Editors, *Let No One Fear Death*

Subdeacon Nektarios Harrison, *Metropolitan Philaret of New York*

Elder George of Grigoriou, *Catholicism in the Light of Orthodoxy*

Archimandrite Ephraim Triandaphillopoulos, *Noetic Prayer as the Basis of Mission and the Struggle Against Heresy*

Dr. Nicholas Baldimtsis, *Life and Witness of St. Iakovos of Evia*

On the Reception of the Heterodox into the Orthodox Church: The Patristic Consensus and Criteria

Patrick (Craig) Truglia, *The Rise and Fall of the Papacy*

St. Raphael of Brooklyn, *In Defense of St. Cyprian*

The Divine Service of the Eighth Œcumenical Council

The Orthodox Patristic Witness Concerning Catholicism

Hieromartyr Seraphim (Svezdinsky), *Homilies on the Divine Liturgy*

Abbe Guettée, *The Papacy*

Select Forthcoming Titles

Cell of the Resurrection, Mount Athos, *On the Mystery of Christ: An Athonite Catechism*

Fr. Theodore Zisis, *Kollyvadica*

George (Pachymeres), *Errors of the Latins*

Fr. George Metallinos, *I Confess One Baptism,* 2nd Edition

St. Maximus the Confessor, *Opuscula: Theological and Polemical Works*

Fr. Peter Heers, *Going Deeper in the Spiritual Life*

Fr. Peter Heers, *On the Body of Christ and Baptism*

Athonite Fathers of the 20th Century, Vol. II

This 1ˢᵗ Edition of

ON THE STEADFASTNESS OF THE ORTHODOX CHURCH

written by St. Raphael of Brooklyn and printed in this two thousand twenty fourth year of our Lord's Holy Incarnation is one of the many fine titles available from Uncut Mountain Press, translators and publishers of Orthodox Christian theological and spiritual literature. Find the book you are looking for at

uncutmountainpress.com

**GLORY BE TO GOD
FOR ALL THINGS**

AMEN.

Made in the USA
Middletown, DE
22 June 2024